A ROMANTIC TREASURY

Letters

Illustrations by Rick Smith

RUNNING PRESS
PHILADELPHIA · LONDON

A Running Press Miniature Edition™
Copyright © 1996 by Running Press.
Illustrations copyright © 1996 by Rick Smith.
Printed in China.

All rights reserved under the Pan-American and
International Copyright Conventions.

*This book may not be reproduced in whole or in part,
in any form or by any means, electronic or mechanical,
including photocopying, recording, or by any information
storage and retrieval system now known or hereafter
invented, without written permission from the publisher.*

*The proprietary trade dress, including the size and format
of this Running Press Miniature Edition™, is the property
of Running Press. It may not be used or reproduced
without the express written permission of Running Press.*

Library of Congress Cataloging-in-Publication Number
95-69319

ISBN 1-56138-689-8

This book may be ordered by mail from the publisher.
Please include $1.00 for postage and handling.
But try your bookstore first!

Running Press Book Publishers
125 South Twenty-second Street
Philadelphia, Pennsylvania 19103-4399

Log onto www.specialfavors.com to order Running Press
Miniature Editions™ with your own custom-made covers!

Visit us on the web!
www.runningpress.com

CONTENTS

Everyone can tell a love letter that has ever received one. One knows them without opening—they are always folded hurriedly and sealed carefully, and the direction manifests a kind of tremulous agitation, that marks the state of the writer's nerves.

—*Sir Walter Scott*

A love letter is the most intimate correspondence a person can receive. Within its lines secret desires are revealed, promises given, and fond memories recalled. Written in elegant script on scented stationery or scrawled haphazardly on a scrap of paper, mailed from across the seas, hidden in a bouquet of roses, or tucked between the pages of an album, a love letter is to be cherished always.

Love letters are precious reminders of heart-felt sentiments. They may bring encouragement and reassurance to the pining heart—"We'll be together soon." Or they may be simple reminders—"I'm thinking about you. You make me smile."

Whatever their purpose, love letters are received with joy and anticipation, then saved in special places—a dresser drawer, under a mattress, ribbon-tied in a hope chest, or secreted away in a quiet corner. They are kept to be lovingly revisited for many years to come.

Over time, letters may become worn and tear-stained, but the meaning of their words remains as true as the day they were written.

Long after lovers are gone, their letters remain. Within these pages are some of the most passionate, poetic, and poignant love letters that have ever been written, read, reread, treasured, and saved forever. Their words echo through the chambers of our hearts. They are intimate yet universal sentiments to be celebrated and shared with the one you love.

to George Sand [Amandine A. L. Dupin]:

I have something stupid and ridiculous to
tell you . . . I am in love with you . . . I
thought I should cure myself in seeing you
quite simply as a friend. . . . But I pay too
dearly for the moments I pass with you. . . .
I know how you think of me, and I have
nothing to hope for in telling you this. I can
only foresee losing a friend and the only
agreeable hours I have passed for a month.
But I know that you are kind, that you have
loved, and I put my trust in you, not as a
mistress, but as a frank and loyal comrade.

—*Alfred de Musset (1810–1857)*

There is only one situation I can think of in which men and women make an effort to read better than they usually do. When they are in love and reading a love letter, they read for all they are worth. They read every word three ways; they read between the lines and in the margins. . . . Then, if never before or after, they read.

—*Mortimer J. Adler (1902–2001)*

Ask the child why it is born; ask the flower why it blossoms, ask the sun why it shines. I love you because I must love you.

— *George Upton (1834–1919)*

This is to let you know
That all I feel for you
Can never wholly go.
I love you and miss you, even two
    hours away,
With all my heart. This is to let
    you know.

—*Noel Coward (1899–1973)*

to Ottoline Morell:

I did not know I loved you till I heard
myself telling you so—for one instant I
thought "Good God, what have I said?"
and then I knew it was the truth.

—*Bertrand Russell (1872–1970)*

to Charmain Kittredge:

. . . . I confess what you already know, what you knew from the very first and from moment to moment through all its changes. But it will relieve me to tell you how my love has greatened. When first I broke the silence, it was with the intention of making you my mistress, or, rather, of trying to make you my mistress. Oh, believe me, believe me, I loved you then, but I loved you so much less than now, because I did not know how much greater you were then as now.

—*Jack London* (1876–1916)

to Maire O'Neill:

Little Heart you don't know how much
feeling I have for you. You are like my
child, and my little wife, and my good
angel, and my greatest friend, all in one!
I don't believe there has been a woman
in Ireland loved the way I love you for a
thousand years.

—*John Millington Synge*
(1871–1909)

to Fanny Brawne:

I never knew before, what such love
as you have me feel, was . . . if you will
fully love me, though there may be some
fire 'twill not be more than we can bear
when moistened and bedewed with
Pleasures. . . . I love you the more in
that I believe you have liked me for my
own sake and for nothing else.

   —*John Keats (1795–1821)*

to Anne Boleyn:

. . . but if it pleases you to do the duty
of a true, loyal mistress and friend, and
to give yourself body and heart to me,
who have been, and will be, your very
loyal servant (if your rigour does not
forbid me), I promise you that not only
the name will be due to you, but also to
take you as my sole mistress, casting off
all others than yourself out of mind and
affection, and to serve you only.

—*Henry VIII (1491–1547)*

A good leg will fail, a straight back will stoop; a black beard will turn white; a curled pate will grow bald; a fair face will wither; a full eye will wax hollow: but a good heart, Kate, is the sun and not the moon; for it shines bright and never changes, but keeps its course truly. If thou would have such a one, take me; and take me, take a soldier, take a soldier, take a king.

—*William Shakespeare (1564–1616)*

But as I love you more than I can express, you will excuse me for making this proposal. I am ready upon these terms to marry you directly. And, upon my honour, I would not propose it now, were I not fully persuaded that I would share a kingdom with you if I had it. I also solemnly promise to do everything in my power to show my gratitude and make you happy.

—*James Boswell* (*1740–1795*)

APR 25 1922

GREEN... 13 JAN 185...

K 8

MARR

To any Minister of the Gospel, Justice of the Peace
You are hereby authorized to join togethe
of your church, society or religious denominati

To be retained by the person solemnizing the marriage

AGE LICENSE

other officers or persons authorized by law to solemnize marriage :
the holy state of matrimony, according to the rites and ceremonies
and the laws of the Commonwealth of Pennsylvania.

of *full age* and *never*
of *Jay Edward Kauffman*

I loved you, so I drew these tides of men into my hands and wrote my will across the sky in stars to earn your freedom, the seven pillared worthy house, that your eyes might be shining for me.

—*[Thomas E.] Lawrence of Arabia (1888–1935)*

You can't think how it cheered me up, this string of communication with you. It felt as if your love was so strong it reached me all the way. I do feel as if there was a lovely and present guardianship all the time; my darling you give me so much more than I deserve. But it does make me feel so quiet and secure.

—*Rupert Brooke (1887–1915)*

to his wife:

My little one, one understands oneself,
I imagine. You will never know exactly
how and how much I love you; nobody
knows it except me. But you almost
know. I kiss you enormously.

—*Arnold Bennett (1867–1931)*

to Woodrow Wilson:

This is my pledge, dearest one, I
will stand by you. . . . And no matter
whether the wine be bitter or sweet we
will share it together and find happiness
in the comradeship.

— *Edith Bolling Galt (1872–1961)*

to Julia Davis:

I feel sad when I don't see you. Be
married, why won't you? And come
to live with me. I will make you as
happy as I can. You shall not be obliged
to work hard; and when you are tired,
you may lie in my lap, and I will sing
you to rest. . . .

—*Zadoc Long (19th century)*

Dost ask (my dear) what service I
    will have?
To love me day and night is all I crave,
To dream on me, to expect, to think
    on me,
Depend and hope, still covet me to see,
Delight thyself in me, but wholly mine,
For know, my love, that I am wholly
    thine.

—*Robert Burton* (*1577–1640*)

to Nicholas II:

Never did I believe there could be such utter happiness in this world, such a feeling of unity between two mortal beings. I love you, those three words have my life in them.

—*Alexandra (1872–1918)*

Afterward we will be as one animal
of the forest and be so close that neither
one can tell that one of us is one and
not the other. Can you not feel my heart
be your heart?

— *Ernest Hemingway (1899–1961)*

to Robert Browning:

And now listen to me in turn. You have touched me more profoundly than I thought even you could have touched me—my heart was full when you came here today. Henceforward I am yours for everything. . . .

—*Elizabeth Barrett Browning*
(1806–1861)

To Elizabeth Barrett Browning:

. . . would I, if I could, supplant one
of any of the affections that I know to
have taken root in you—that great and
solemn one, for instance. I feel that if I
could get myself remade, as if turned to
gold, I WOULD not even then desire
to become more than the mere setting to
that diamond you must always wear.
The regard and esteem you now give me,
in this letter, and which I press to my
heart and bow my head upon, is all I
can take and all too embarrassing, using
all my gratitude.

—*Robert Browning (1812–1889)*

I will make you brooches and toys for
  your delight
Of bird-song at morning and star-shine
  at night.
I will build a palace fit for you and me,
Of green days in forests and blue days
  at sea. . . .

And this shall be for music when no one
  else is near,
The fine song for singing, the rare song
  to hear!
That only I remember, that only you admire,
Of the broad road that stretches and the
  roadside fire.

    —Robert Louis Stevenson (1850–1894)

to Elizabeth Wilson:

I go about murmuring, "I have made that dignified girl commit herself, I have," and then I vault over the sofa with exultation.

— *Walter Bagehot (1826–1877)*

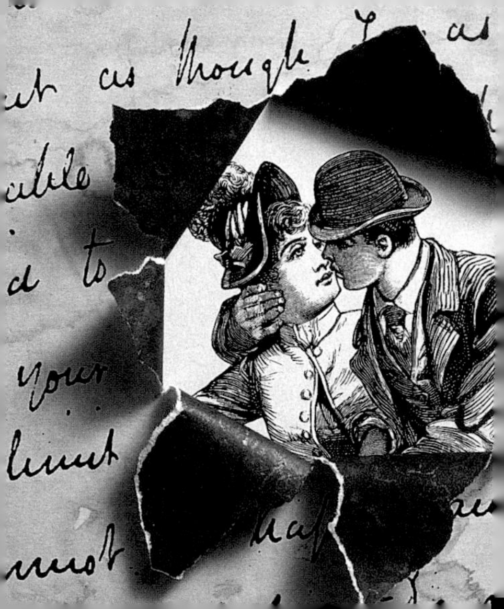

cupous

of soon seeing you

far from you..

My love

Power of

you Love

the at us even

to Fanny Brawne:

I cannot exist without you—I am forgetful
of every thing but seeing you again—my
Life seems to stop there—I see no further.
You have absorb'd me. I have a sensation
at the present moment as though I were
dissolving. . . . I have been astonished that
Men could die Martyrs for religion—I have
shudder'd at it —I shudder no more—I
could be martyr'd for my Religion—Love
is my religion—I could die for that—I
could die for you. My creed is Love and
you are its only tenet—You have ravish'd
me away by a Power I cannot resist.

—*John Keats (1795–1821)*

All that you are, all that I owe to you,
justifies my love, and nothing, not even
you, would keep me from adoring you.

— *Marquis de Lafayette (1757–1834)*

to Felice Bauer:

. . . but my heart beats through my
entire body and is conscious only of you.
I belong to you; there is really no other
way of expressing it, and that is not
strong enough.

—*Franz Kafka (1883–1924)*

about Elizabeth Paul:

My torn feet were touched by the golden
dust of the road. My fingers tore at the
gold and silver gown that wrapped her
about. With a little whispering laugh she
passed into me. I was drawn into her and
was healed.

—*Sherwood Anderson (1876–1941)*

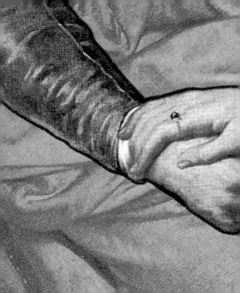

There is one thing of which I am so sure
that nothing will ever change it—that
you will always be exquisitely lovable—
whether I win you or not—I have given
my heart to one of God's finest crea-
tures—that every thought and memory
of you will be sweet and gentle. . . . I
have done myself the highest possible
honor in giving you my heart.

—*Vachel Lindsay (1879–1931)*

to Edith Bolling Galt:

The way you let your hand rest in mine, my bewitching Sweetheart, fills me with happiness. It is the perfection of confiding love. Everything you do, the little unconscious instinctive things in particular, charms me and increases my sense of nearness to you, identification with you, till my heart is full to overflowing.

— *Woodrow Wilson (1856–1924)*

to Ellen Terry:

I love you soulfully and bodyfully,
properly and improperly, every way
that a woman can be loved.

— *George Bernard Shaw (1856–1950)*

to Clara Schumann:

My beloved Clara, I wish I could write to
you as tenderly as I love you and tell you
all the good things that I wish you. You
are so infinitely dear to me, dearer than
I can say. I should like to spend the whole
day calling you endearing names and pay-
ing you compliments without ever being
satisfied. If things go on much longer
as they are at present I shall have, some
time, to put you under glass or to have
you set in gold.

—*Johannes Brahms (1833–1897)*

to Arabella Hunt:

In the midst of crowds I remain in solitude. Nothing but you can lay hold of my mind, and that can lay hold of nothing but you. I appear transported to some foreign desert with you . . . where, abundantly supplied with everything . . . I might live out an age of uninterrupted ecstasy . . . the charms of all the world appear to be translated to thee.

— *William Congreve (1670–1729)*

to Augusta McKim:

O happy hours when I may once more
encircle within these arms the dearest
object of my love—when I shall again feel
the pressure of that "aching head" which
will delight to recline upon my bosom,
when I may again press to my heart which
palpitates with the purest affection that
loved one who has so long shared its
undivided devotion.

*—Alexander Hamilton Rice
(19th century)*

to Lady Emerald Cunard:

The hours I spend with you I look upon
as a sort of perfumed garden, a dim
twilight, and a fountain singing to it . . .
you and you alone make me feel that I
am alive. . . . Other men it is said have
seen angels, but I have seen thee and
thou art enough.

—*George Moore (1852–1933)*

to Olivia Langdon:

Livy dear, I have already mailed today's
letter, but I am so proud of my privilege
of writing the dearest girl in the world
whenever I please, that I must add a few
lines if only to say I love you, Livy. For
I do love you, Livy—as the dew loves the
flowers; as the birds love the sunshine; as
the wavelets love the breeze; as mothers
love their first-born; as memory loves old
faces; as the yearning tides love the moon;
as the angels love the pure in heart. . . .

— *Samuel Clemens (1835–1910)*

to Lilian Paula Steichen:

Ten thousand love-birds, sweet throated
and red-plumed, were in my soul, in the
garden of my under-life. There on ten
thousand branches they slept as in night-
time. You came and they awoke. . . . a
dawn burst on them—a long night was
ended. God! how they sang. . . . These
birds want freedom. . . . But I can let out
only one at a time. Each letter, then, is
some joy till now jailed—but now sent
flying—and flying and flying!

—*Carl Sandburg (1878–1967)*

How many times do I love thee, dear?
Tell me how many thoughts there be
In the atmosphere
Of a new fall'n year. . . .

— *Thomas Lovell Beddoes*
  (1803–1849)

to Victorien Sardou:

Your words are my food, your breath my wine. You are everything to me.

—*Sarah Bernhardt (1844–1923)*

to Mrs. Wyndham Lewis:

I am mad with love. My passion is frenzy.
The respect of our immediate meeting
overwhelms and entrances me. I pass my
nights and days in scenes of strange and
fascinating rapture. . . .

—*Benjamin Disraeli (1804–1881)*

to Vita Sackville-West:

Heavens above! The reason why I'm so jealous of you is obvious enough! If you weren't so damned attractive physically, do you think my heart would beat almost to suffocation whenever I see you speak to someone?

If you don't realize how attractive you are in that way, let me tell you, other people do, and have told me so. . . .

— *Violet Trefussis (1894–1972)*

to Katherine Mansfield:

There's only one thing greater than my
fear—that is my love. My love will
always conquer my fear—but it can't do
it immediately. It needs the full force of
my love to do it and it takes days for that
to emerge out of its dark hiding places.

—*John Middleton Murry*
(1889–1956)

to John Middleton Murry:

I have loved you for three years with my heart and my mind, but it seems to me I have never loved you *avec mon âme,* as I do now. I love you with all our future life—our life together which seems only now to have taken root and to be alive and growing up in the sun. . . . I have never felt anything like it before. In fact I did not comprehend the possibility of such a thing.

—*Katherine Mansfield (1888–1923)*

I don't love you as if you were the
    salt-rose, topaz
or arrow of carnations that propagate
    fire:
I love you as certain dark things are
    loved,
secretly, between the shadow and the
    soul.

I love you as the plant that doesn't
    bloom and carries
hidden within itself the light of those
    flowers,
and thanks to your love, darkly in
    my body

lives the dense fragrance that rises
    from the earth.

I love you without knowing how, or
    when, or from where,
I love you simply, without problems
    or pride:
I love you in this way because I don't
    know any other way of loving
but this, in which there is no I or you,
so intimate that your hand upon my
    chest is my hand,
so intimate that when I fall asleep it is
    your eyes that close.

   —Pablo Neruda (1904–1973)

without

separate

heart

to Peter Abélard:

I have your picture in my room. I never pass by it without stopping to look at it; and yet when you were present with me, I scarce ever cast my eyes upon it. If a picture which is but a mute representation of an object can give such pleasure, what cannot letters inspire? They have souls, they can speak, they have in them all that force which expresses the transport of the heart; they have all the fire of our passions. . . .

—*Héloise (c. 1098–1164)*

to Héloise:

. . . I propose now to dry up those tears which the sad description occasioned you to shed; I intend to mix my grief with yours, and pour out my heart before you: in short, to lay open before your eyes all my trouble, and the secret of my soul, which my vanity has hitherto made me conceal from the rest of the world. . . .

   —*Peter Abélard (1079–c. 1144)*

to Walt Whitman:

All—all to me speak of thee Dear Walt.—
Seeing them my friend the part thou
occupiest in my spiritual nature—I feel
assured you will forgive my remissness of
me in writing—My love my Walt—is with
you always.

—*Fred Vaughn (19th century)*

The feeling of separation,
    what is there to say
But that the heart
    is an endless river of stars.

— *Wen T'ing-yün (c. 813-870)*

to Olympe Dunoyer:

I am a prisoner here in the name of the King; they can take my life, but not the love that I feel for you. . . . No, nothing has the power to part me from you; our love is based upon virtue, and will last as long as our lives, Adieu, there is nothing that I will not brave for your sake. . . .

—*Voltaire (1694–1798)*

to Joséphine Bonaparte:

A few days ago I thought I loved you;
but since I last saw you I feel I love you
a thousand times more. All the time I
have known you I adore you more each
day; that just shows how wrong was
La Bruyère's maxim that *love comes all
at once.* Everything in Nature has its
own life and different stages of growth.
I beg you, let me see some of your faults:
be less beautiful, less graceful, less kind,
less good. . . .

—*Napoléon Bonaparte (1769–1821)*

to Mary Wordsworth:

How do I long to tread for the first time
the road that will bring me in sight of
Grasmere . . . to see to touch you to speak
to you and hear you speak. . . . Fail not
to write to me . . . let me not then be
disappointed, but give me your heart that
I may kiss the words a thousand times!

—*William Wordsworth (1770–1850)*

to Virginia Woolf:

. . . I miss you even more than I could have believed; and I was prepared to miss you a good deal. So this letter is just really a squeal of pain. It is incredible how essential to me you have become. I suppose you are accustomed to people saying these things. Damn you, spoilt creature; I shan't make you love me any more by giving myself away like this—But oh my dear, I can't be clever and stand-offish with you: I love you too much for that.

—*Vita Sackville-West (1892–1962)*

But soft! sink low!
Soft! let me just murmur,
And do you wait a moment you husky-
nois'd sea,
For somewhere I believe I hear my mate
responding to me,
So faint, I must be still, be still to listen,
But not altogether still, for then she might
not come
immediately to me.

Hither my love!
Here I am! here!
With this just-sustain'd note I announce
myself to you,
This gentle call is for you my love, for you.

— *Walt Whitman (1819–1892)*

Oh, what good will writing do? I want
to put my hand out and touch you. I
want to do for you and care for you. I
want to be there when you're sick and
when you're lonesome.

—*Edith Wharton (1862–1937)*

to Lady Diana Manners:

. . . I find that I miss you most inconveniently and the thought of not seeing you at champagne-time is as exasperating as it would be for the moth to miss his candle of an evening.

—*Alfred Duff Cooper (1890–1954)*

Reminis

cences

to Jean-Paul Sartre:

My love, I never felt our love more strongly than that evening at Les Vikings, where you gazed at me so tenderly I felt like weeping. . . . If I weren't so uncomfortably positioned for writing, I'd spend pages telling you how happy I am and how much I love you. But I take comfort from the fact that you felt it clearly yourself, didn't you, little man? Here are a hundred kisses, each carrying the same message.

— *Simone de Beauvoir (1908–1986)*

to Joséphine Bonaparte:

Your letter has been a balm to me. Be happy; be as happy as you deserve to be; it is my whole heart that speaks. You have given me my share, too, of happiness, and a share very keenly felt; nothing else can have for me the value of a token of remembrance.

—*Napoléon Bonaparte (1769–1821)*

to Louise Colet:

. . . what memories! And what desire!
Ah! Our two marvelous carriage rides;
how beautiful they were, particularly the
second, with the lightning flashes above
us. I keep remembering the color of the
trees lit by the streetlights, and the sway-
ing motion of the springs. We were alone,
happy: I kept staring at you, and even
in the darkness your whole face seemed
illumined by your eyes.

—*Gustave Flaubert (1821–1880)*

to Sarah Helen Whitman:

Yes, I now feel that it was then on that evening of sweet dreams—that the very first dawn of human love burst upon the icy night of my spirit. Since that period I have never seen nor heard your name without a shiver half of delight, half of anxiety. . . . For years your name never passed my lips, while my soul drank in, with a delirious thirst, all that was uttered in my presence respecting you.

—*Edgar Allan Poe (1809–1849)*

Edgar Allan Poe

about Edward VIII:

This was our Eden. . . . I found myself
swept from the accustomed mooring of
caution. Each night I felt more completely
possessed by our love, carried ever more
swiftly into uncharted seas of feeling,
content to let the Prince chart the course,
heedless of where the voyage would end.

— *Thelma Furness (20th century)*

If I am pressed to say why I loved him, I feel it can only be explained by replying: "Because it was he; because it was me."

—*Michel de Montaigne (1533–1592)*

Time and space and body were the very things that brought us together; the telephone wires by which we communicated.

—*C. S. Lewis (1898–1963)*

And indeed I felt happy with her, so perfectly happy, that the one desire of my mind was that it should differ in nothing from hers, and already I wished for nothing beyond her smile, and to walk with her thus, hand in hand, along a sun-warmed, flower-bordered path.

—*André Gide (1869–1951)*

to his wife:

We parted manfully and womanfully as we ought. I drank only half a bottle of the Rhine wine, and only the half of that, ere I fell asleep on the sofa, which lasted two hours. It was the reaction, for your going tired me more than I cared to show. Then I drank the other half, and as that did not do, I went and retraced our walk in the park, and sat down in the same seat, and felt happier and better.

— *Thomas Hood (1799–1845)*

I fell in love with her courage, her sincerity, and her flaming self-respect and it's these things I'd believe in even if the whole world indulged in wild suspicions that she wasn't all she should be. . . . I love her and that's the beginning of everything.

—*F. Scott Fitzgerald (1896–1940)*

w loves the flowers

s love the sunsh

let love the

to Percy Bysshe Shelley:

How you reason & philosophize about love—do you know if I had been asked I could not have given one reason in its favour—yet I have as great an opinion as you concerning its exaltedness and love very tenderly to prove my theory—adieu for the present. . . .

—*Mary Shelley (1797–1851)*

about Elinor Frost:

She has been the unspoken half of
everything I ever wrote, and both
halves of many a thing. . . .

—*Robert Frost (1874–1963)*

about Abraham Lincoln:

To love and to cherish. It was always music in my ears, both before and after our marriage, when my husband told me that I was the only one, he had ever thought of, or cared for.

—*Mary Todd Lincoln (1818–1882)*

So touch the air softly,
And swing the broom high.
We will dust the gray mountains,
And sweep the blue sky;
And I'll love you as long
As the furrow the plow,
And However is Ever,
And Ever is Now.

—*William Jay Smith (b. 1918)*

to Madame Denis:

Sensual pleasure passes and vanishes in the twinkling of an eye, but the friendship between us, the mutual confidence, the delights of the heart, the enchantment of the soul, these things do not perish and can never be destroyed. I shall love you until I die.

—*Voltaire (1694-1778)*

to Lucia Elizabeth Vestris:

My own dearest beloved wife—your reminder of our wedding day brought the tears into my eyes; for though I may be inattentive to such anniversaries generally, my heart must be made of stone not to care, to mind and contrast the happiness experienced on that blessed day. . . . Believe me, my darling, Lizzie, when I swear that my love for you is as true at this moment as it was eighteen years ago.

    —Charles James Matthews
    (1803–1878)

to Harold Nicolson:

You are dearer to me than anybody ever has been or ever could be. . . . I do not think one could conceive of a love more exclusive, more tender, or more pure than I have for you. I think it is immortal, a thing which happens seldom.

. . . there are not many people who would write such a letter after sixteen years of marriage. . . . I sometimes try to tell you the truth, and then I find that I have no words at my command which could possibly convey it to you.

—*Vita Sackville-West (1892–1962)*

to Nora Barnstable:

Anyhow, Nora, I love you. I cannot live
without you. I would like to give you everything that is mine. . . . telling you more
and more until we grew to be one being
together until the hour should come for us
to die. Even now the tears rush to my eyes
and sobs choke my throat as I write
this. . . . bear with me a little even if I am
inconsiderate and unmanageable and believe me we will be happy together. Let me
love you in my own way. Let me have your
heart always close to mine to hear every
throb of my life, every sorrow, every joy.

—*James Joyce (1882–1941)*

to "Anthea":

Thou art my life, my love, my heart,
   The very eyes of me:
And hast command of every part,
   To live and die for thee.

    —*Robert Herrick (1591–1674)*

to Anaïs Nin:

You make me tremendously happy to
hold me undivided—to let me be the artist,
as it were, and yet not forgo the man. . . .
No woman has ever granted me all the
privileges I need—and you, why you sing
out so blithely, so boldly, with a laugh
even—yes, you invite me to go ahead, be
myself, venture anything. I adore you for
that. That is where you are truly regal, a
woman extraordinary.

—*Henry Miller (1891–1980)*

to Henry Miller:

When you are thoughtful and moving,
I lose my mind. To stay with you for one
night I would throw away my whole life,
sacrifice a hundred persons, I would burn
Louveciennes, be capable of *anything*.
This is not to worry you, Henry, it is just
that I can't keep from saying it, that I am
overflowing, desperately in love with you
as I never was with anyone.

—*Anaïs Nin (1903–1977)*

to F. Scott Fitzgerald:

Don't ever think of the things you can't give me—You've trusted me with the dearest heart of all—and it's so damn much more than anybody else in the world has ever had.

—*Zelda Sayre Fitzgerald*
(1900–1948)

to Clementine Churchill:

. . . my chief desire is to link myself to you week by week by bonds which shall ever become more intimate and profound. Beloved I kiss your memory—your sweetness and beauty have cast a glory upon my life.

— Winston Churchill (1874–1965)

Winston S. Churchill

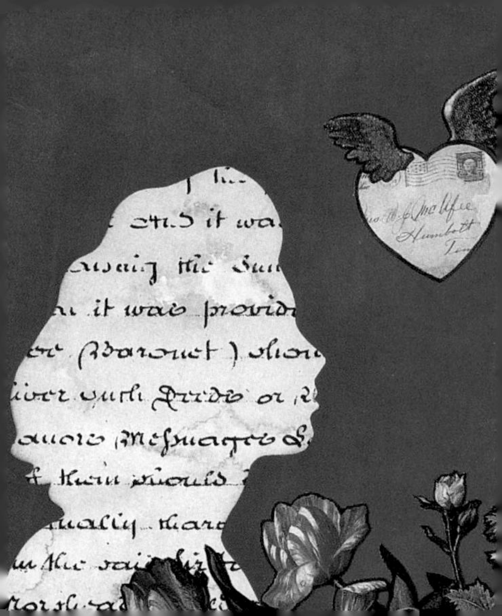

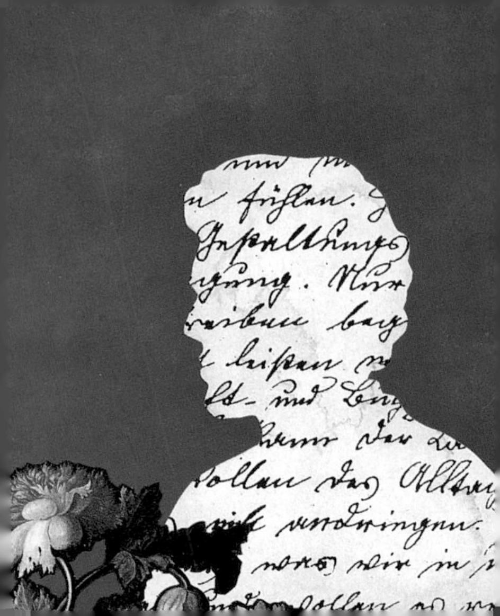

to the "Immortal Beloved":

Be calm, only by a calm consideration
of our existence can we achieve our
purpose to live together—be calm—love
me—today—yesterday—what tearful
longings for you—you—you—my life—
my all—farewell—Oh continue to love
me—never misjudge the most faithful
heart of your beloved I.

 ever thine

 ever mine

 ever for each other

 —*Ludwig van Beethoven*
 (1700–1827)

to Countess Nadezhda Von Meck:

. . . no one in the world could respond
more keenly to the deepest and most
secret gropings of my soul. No musical
dedication has ever been more seriously
meant. It was spoken not only on my
part but on yours; the symphony was not,
in truth, mine but ours.

—*Pyotr Ilich Tchaikovsky
(1840–1893)*

When our two souls stand up
   erect and strong,
Face to face, silent, drawing
   nigh and nigher,
Until the lengthening wings
   break into fire
At either curved point,
   —what bitter wrong
Can the earth do us,
   that we should not long
Be here contented! Think. In
   mounting higher,

The angels would press on us
    and aspire
To drop some golden orb of
    perfect song
Into our deep, dear silence. Let us stay
Rather on earth, Beloved—where
    the unfit
Contrarious moods of men recoil away
And isolate pure spirits, and permit
A place to stand and love in for a day . . .

  —*Elizabeth Barrett Browning*
  (1806–1861)

. . . verily love knows not 'mine'
  or 'thine;'
With separate 'I' and 'thou' free love
  had done,
      For one is both and both are one
      in love:
Rich love knows nought of 'think that
  is not mine;'
          Both have the strength and both
          the length thereof,
Both of us, of the love which makes
  us one.

  —*Christina Rossetti (1830–1894)*

Believe me, if all those endearing
   young charms,
      Which I gaze on so fondly today,
Were to change by tomorrow, and fleet
   in my arms. . .
Thou wouldst still be adored, as this
   moment thou art,
      Let thy loveliness fade as it will,
And around the dear ruin each wish
   of my heart
      Would entwine itself verdantly still.

—*Thomas Moore (1779–1852)*

to Countess Guiccioli:

You will not understand these English words, and others will not understand them. . . . But you will recognize the handwriting of him who passionately loved you, and you will divine that, over a book which was yours, he could only think of love. . . . I love you, and you love me,—at least, you say so, and act as if you did so, which last is a great consolation in all events. But I more than love you, and cannot cease to love you.

— *George Gordon, Lord Byron*
(1788–1824)

about "Annabel Lee":

And neither the angels in Heaven above
    Nor the demons down under the sea,
Can ever dissever my soul from the soul
    Of the beautiful Annabel Lee. . . .

—*Edgar Allan Poe (1809–1849)*

to Sophia Hawthorne:

Yes; but you will be the same to me,
because we have met in Eternity, and
there our intimacy was formed

— *Nathaniel Hawthorne (1804–1864)*

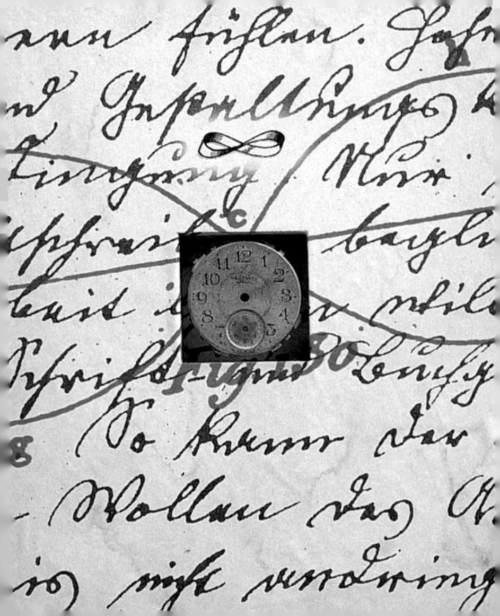

to her husband:

If ever two were one, then surely we.
If ever man were lov'd by wife, then thee;
If ever wife was happy in a man,
Compare with me ye women if you can. . . .
My love is such that Rivers cannot quench,
Nor ought but love from thee give
   recompence.
Thy love is such I can no way repay,
The heavens reward thee manifold I pray.
Then while we live, in love let's so persever,
That when we live no more,
   we may live ever.

—*Anne Bradstreet (c. 1612–1672)*

I'll love you till the ocean
  Is folded and hung up to dry,
And the seven stars go squawking
  Like geese about the sky.

The years shall run like rabbits,
  For in my arms I hold
The Flower of the Ages,
  And the first love of the world.
  — *W. H. Auden (1907–1973)*

Had I no eyes but ears,
  my ears would love
That inward beauty and invisible;
Or were I deaf, thy outward parts
  would move
Each part in me that were but sensible:
    Though neither eyes nor ears,
      to hear nor see,
    Yet I should be in love
      by touching thee.
Say that the sense of feeling
  were bereft me,

And that I could not see, nor hear,
  nor touch,
And nothing but the very smell
  were left me,
Yet would my love to thee be still
  as much;
    For from the stillitory of
      thy face excelling
    Comes breath perfumed,
      that breedeth love by smelling.

—*William Shakespeare* (1564–1616)

Acknowledge

Excerpt from "As I Walked Out One Evening," *Collected Poems* by W. H. Auden, edited by Edward Mendelson. Copyright © 1940 and renewed 1968 by W. H. Auden. Reprinted by permission of Random House, Inc. Reprinted by permission of Faber & Faber, Ltd.

Excerpt from "This Is to Let You Know" by Noel Coward. *Noel Coward: Collected Verse*, Methuen, 1984. Collection copyright © 1984 by the Estate of the late Noel Coward. Reprinted by permission of Reed Books, London.

"Sonnet XVII" by Pablo Neruda/Translated by S. Mitchell from *Into the Garden: A Wedding Anthology* by Robert Hass and Stephen Mitchell. Copyright © 1993 by Robert Hass and Stephen Mitchell. Translation copyright © 1993 by Stephen Mitchell. Reprinted by permission of HarperCollins Publishers, Inc.

Excerpt from *The Letters of Carl Sandburg*, copyright © 1968 by Lilian Steichen Sandburg, Trustee, reprinted by permission of Harcourt Brace & Company.

Excerpt from *Collected Poems 1939–1989: William Jay Smith*, Charles Scribner's Sons, copyright © 1960, 1995 by William Jay Smith. Reprinted by permission of the author.

Special thanks to:

Charles Roberts Autograph Letters Collection, Haverford College Library. [Letter from John Keats to Fanny Browne]: pp. 40–41; p. 58 (details: right); p. 66–67

Mark Twain, MARK TWAIN'S LETTERS. VOL. 3: 1869. Edited/translated by Victor Fischer. Copyright © 1992 The Mark Twain Foundation. Published by arrangement with University of California Press. [Letter from Samuel Clemens to Olivia Langdon]: p. 58 (details: top left and left); p. 77; p. 94; endpapers (detail)

Signatures from the Ray Rawlins Collection: p. 18; p. 24; p. 28; p. 35; p. 36; p. 87; p. 112; p. 113; p. 119; pp. 124–125; endpapers (details)

Signatures provided by Helen and George Sanders, Autograph House: p. 17; p. 43; p. 49; p. 50; p. 55; p. 56; p. 60; p. 75; p. 85; p. 90; p. 93; p. 96; p. 104; p. 106; p. 107; p. 109; endpapers (details)

Additional photographs and letters provided by the Van Horn family.

This book has been bound
using handcraft methods,
and Smyth-sewn to ensure durability.

The cover and interior were designed
by Frances J. Soo Ping Chow.

The text was edited
by Tara Ann McFadden.

Picture research by Susan Oyama.

The text was set in Sabon and Serlio.

esource it is a nice Work.

back to Fürth than we had a verry nice Time.
ght and I am still always funny.
he Town is a club and evry night Dance.It is
neat like in Fürth.You should see saw the Club
y have remembled it.They p...led Picture as th
fixed cup.Table and the Chair is red.Oh th
arious Picture that that you are aet here.We ha
ot than you here home and have a nice Time in yo
n the B.P...... and working.it is 20:00 hours
y to 22:00 ....fter you left from Fürthal a
out 4 more and .... Jimmy wrote me a letter to
I take off .....e Town and I am now here.
you soon ....e and if I ever come to America I'll
id my Jimmy about you and he say's it is always
he Truth.You know that I wont lie.
...think back some times to Germany and dont forget
y Jimmy's Address and if you want to write back
to Jimmy.Here are my your Letter.
alls to Herb..f you and him some times.
So all for this time.

Hallo and be good like I do always!

Carl Sandburg

Heidelberg
1896

Din Linken zu ...
Tag Leben, Tag ...